Every Kinda Lady

Monologues in Poetry
(Volume 1)

By
Nzima

Production design by John Sheirer.

ISBN: 978-1537415918

Enfield, Connecticut
www.everykindalady.com

About the Poet

Nzima states that her poetry, short stories, quotes, and expressive writing comes from life's upheavals, the hurt places, as well as the thankful, growing and feel good memorable places. Nzima states that it is impossible for her to live her life without accepting her whole self and to be married to all of her yesterday's thoughts and beliefs. She resents any and all systems or entities telling her what time it is. She feels it is a form of oppression. One form of freedom as stated by Nzima is to write without worrying about what others may think…Thus, birthed a quote about time "Don't try and change time". Do not try and edit past self, journeys, truths, feelings, journals and rhythms...leave it alone. Nzima has done collaborative work, performances and read-ins with various social groups, and community organizations. Nzima participates in the Freshwater poetry festival, Black History Month read-ins, and Poetry for Peace read-ins. Nzima is also an expressive writing coach, and the founder and organizer of the Every Kind Lady Company, an all-women's expressive writing and Poetry Company. Nzima host workshops and writing circles. A collaboration she holds dear to her heart was with her sister Nicole Rene Roberson, and her stage play Falling Stars on Shantis Bridge, her Poem (Unsettling, Thems & Theys) received a live debut in 2015. Early Publication can be found in *Nota Bene 2010*, the Phi Theta Kappa Honor Society Anthology. The poem was untitled. The poems, "God Why My Flower Child" and "Eight," appeared in the *Freshwater Poetry Journal*, under her full birth name, slave name Sherylle D. Roberson Hutchings in 2009 and 2010.

Poems

- ❖ Every Kinda Lady
- ❖ Never Did He Grab His Gun
- ❖ Losing Hands
- ❖ Missing Smiles
- ❖ Frontin in the Midst of my Survivin
- ❖ Verses Sitting Dormant
- ❖ Selling Hurt
- ❖ I See You
- ❖ Free Style meetings
- ❖ Blue Black and Brown Beautiful
- ❖ Beautiful She
- ❖ Walked
- ❖ Colorful She
- ❖ Permanent Recesses
- ❖ Young Lady in Waiting
- ❖ Moments of Silence (Part 1)
- ❖ Moments of Silence (Part 2)
- ❖ Moments of Silence (Part 3)
- ❖ Women to Women
- ❖ A Rose
- ❖ I Gave
- ❖ Everything
- ❖ When a Purse Becomes a Bag
- ❖ Same Man
- ❖ Momma Morning Saga
- ❖ Fireflies
- ❖ Denied in Writing
- ❖ Lie
- ❖ Free Me
- ❖ Residue
- ❖ Who
- ❖ Ah Piece
- ❖ A Divorcee Testimony
- ❖ Grandmas' Dust Pan
- ❖ I Ain't

- ❖ Living Poetry
- ❖ Who Letcha Out
- ❖ Being Natural
- ❖ Forward Moving
- ❖ Pockets
- ❖ A Boy Needs
- ❖ Lady to Lady
- ❖ Air of Self
- ❖ Loss Womb
- ❖ Folks and their Daughters
- ❖ Still Standing
- ❖ A Sister Keeper Mission

Short Stories

- ❖ She Stare Out the Window
  Includes Poems:
  God Why My Flower Child
  Our Story

- ❖ The Fixed Honey Brown Perm Box Lady
  Includes Poems:
  Black Like Me
  Original By Design

Quotes

- ❖ Quotes
- ❖ Quotes with Questions and Thinking Prompts

A Birthday Haiku for Knia 2017

Dedication: To all the ladies...

Who gave birth to my aesthetics. To the women who loved &
love me, combed my thick hair as a girl and lived to complain
about it, brought me my first bra, stayed in the birthing room with
me, taught me how to carry myself, listened to my heart, and
supported me in my endeavors. To the women that gave me their
awkward truths and un-edited honesty, so I can free mine. To the
women that told me when I was being beautiful & ugly. To my
favorite young lady, the most resilient, beautiful, kindest and
precious young lady in my world, my flower child, my
inspiration, my sunshine and poetry, Knia Khaye Hutchings.

Author's Note

The compilations and inspiration for these poems are partly based on real life narratives, observations and stories of women that crossed my path, my own personal experiences and thoughts throughout the years, and yes… imagination too. As an expressive writing coach and poet, I encourage people to write about their traumas, fears, secrets, unedited truths, injustices, affirmations, observations, thoughts, trials, successes and dreams…to go for it all, to go raw, to kick down any and all walls…to get what they want and need by writing it out…

Introduction

The desire to like, love and accept my whole self in whatever state I'm in, to let go of the slave tongue and the acquiescent sagas has made me question myself. In addition, it inspired my expressive writing to keep a journal, and to express my thoughts poetically, I decided to get real with myself, as well as, pay attention to myself and my surroundings by looking inwardly and out and taking notes (real notes)… the factual beauty and bull sh*t were beyond belief, overwhelming! I felt a need to lay out what make sense to me. Furthermore, I think there would be less confusion in the world if people communicated with themselves and think a little more for themselves and to listen and respect their private thoughts.

Epiphanies and several random profound thoughts, viewpoints, and clarity would fill my head, while alone, in my peaceful space…some life changing thoughts were birthed while sipping tea unclothed in the quiet stillness of my home, a mom & pop café, commuting alone on a train, walking alongside of the Connecticut river, camping, gardening, painting, and relaxing in bed late at night. I now carry my laptop or journal everywhere I go. I highly recommend it. Thus, I use to write my thoughts down on anything; such as the back of a receipt, scrap paper or text it to myself, once I wrote on the inside of a piece of dried bark I found on the ground, because I didn't want to forget my thought along with the setting and energy that came along with it.

Gardening, which I love, became even more interesting and political…I would debate the benefits, beauty, and belonging of dandelions in my flowerbeds. I saw myself as the dandelion. Moreover, I now consider dandelions to be a flower and tea garnish with benefits, as a child I called it a wishing flower. F.Y.I,, according to some research studies and the earthy crunchy conscious folks, dandelions are very rich in vitamins, fiber, iron, and are perfect in tea and more…disclaimer alert: (I am not a doctor, herbalist or nutritionist). Seems like a lot of things unwanted or hard to regulate are considered a weed or used as scare tactics. Thinking and researching works!

Too often people keep things all bottled up... Often suffocating by compromising truths. I say open up those bottled emotions, share it, if only a note to self. Put the message in physical bottle and let it flow. Once we open up, it allows honesty to step in, and encourage affirming approaches to life. Moreover, keeping a journal, or engaging in expressive writing helps to document growth, as well as, being therapeutic, which gives one a safe and non-judgmental space. Consequently, we become authors and inspirations in our own lives and others.

There are things we think we know about ourselves until a situation arises. We surprise ourselves, and find out who we are when caught in raw unrehearsed moments...which fuels the awkward real truths about who we are. Self-discovery by doing some analysis is indeed a journey everyone needs to take. The journey is an extensive, unending, sometimes loaded and brutal journey. Thankfully, it is a journey where all or some of the baggage could be left behind if desired. Thinking, questioning, answering, learning, challenging and taking notes (mental and physical) are crucial. Although, I discovered a lot, I am still looking for my traveling shoes in my journey. The Every Kinda Lady Poem, is the foundation of many things in my past and current life.

A Haiku Dedication

for Knia

Knia I miss you...
Twenty seventeen I am
doing it for you.

Every Kinda Lady

Constancy is an unfair brand of a lady
See I   I Think I've been   every kinda   lady
her and her and   her too

The kind I   didn't understand
the kind I   feared envied   yet I   revered

the kind I   might've shamed   wouldn't claim
the kinda lady I   gotta be.
Yes, even that girl   her and her and   her too

The kind I   couldn't stand or   even forgive
The kinda lady that both lived   and survived

The kind I grieved   the kind I   I prayed heavily to be
The kinda lady I   gotta to be
Yes   every kind   even she…

Never Did he Grab his Gun

He said he would always love and protect me. Never did he grab his gun.

He sent me to work to help make ends meet so we could buy bread. I agreed. The children needed to be fed. Pressing sheets in the factory shop was the labor I was being meagerly paid for... but, yet made to owe debts to the boss, and younger, not yet breasted girls I didn't know. Protecting them steadied me, as my boss mounted and pushed mops n brooms in me, POW! Shove... face down, legs spread. I retreated.

I retreated against my body n soul's permission...

Olive branches, doves, coffins, and him being dead is what my soul   kept wishin...
My - my husband said he would always love and protect me, but he kept on pushing me out the front door. Being poor, a woman and violated was too redundant to report. Neva mind being Negro, dealing with Jim crow...
like window dressings showcased at stores, our reality of what is believed & sold and what is lived must not be seen, just somberly stowed. So, again and again and again...my husband's position and desperation overruled me, his hands and shame almost killed me. Yet again, just the same, I was made to maintain the frontline.

The children needed to be fed. So he pushed me out...out the front door.

Pow! All is dead now. I had to be the one. Never did he grab his gun.

Loosing Hands

We gambled our hands and ties, knowing we were bound to loose site of reality. We operated carelessly on our desires and compassions. We tested scientific theories, as our history remains a misery woven in complacency …we regulated and reallocated each other's Serotonin and Dopamine levels and needs. By all means we retreated and proceeded out of bounds. Time was powerless against us, as it fell into a state of comatose, as we plugged out of our voids and into our feel goods, the vulnerable and romantics. Call it a respite. Call it a time to toast...we never could figure or confer the semantics or math…just knew we should never boast or write it down on paper. It was far too much, to abstract. From the start our loss was when we artfully climbed in and out of our real forms, and failing to end acts and our other situations. Traces of hope and denial had a hand in that part. Nevertheless, we repositioned and discovered how to rearrange our perceptual furniture pieces. We returned our nuptials as they were, picked up our moral grounds, and moved each other's truths around a bit. As we let go winning gains, hands, and ties… our handlings posed indiscriminate conflicts, our   everything inside died   as our lips parted and hearts   pretended to say goodbye.

Missing Smile

She can't seem to find her smile at the bottom of her glass anymore. After she lifts her head and neck out of that bin, she shuts her eyes and drops down her chin again... imaginin' if she can't see out, no one could see in. Her grace once framed the most envious stares in other women. From the sight of her grin men's hearts useta lit in sin, and buy her a fine wine or gin. She use to be first in her class, first class, a lady with a jazz- Slices of limes, salted rimmed glasses, green olives, and cherries, adorned the kiss of her lips, and nothing could ever tame the dance or curve of her hips. Now her profile mirrors x-rays, filled with negative spaces. Everyone now in her graces pity her storyline told in her face and turn their faces. She can't seem to find her smile at the bottom of her glass anymore. After she lifts her head and neck out of that bin, she shuts her eyes and drops down her chin again, imaginin' if she can't see out, no one could see in. She was the kinda lady with a song in her stride and if the blues was at play nobody ever knew. She'd hide the bad alongside nips of jack, coniyac, bourbon within her bright colored bags... reds, purples, and blues

---

14

Frontin In the Midst of My Survivin

My situation got the 1st of the month
lookn like the end of the month.
Yup I be frontin in the midst of my survivin.
Cat-walkin down aisles   head high   heels on
upping up the antics   pimpin out shoppin wagons
with my favorite organics' mangoes and pomegranates
grapes and cherry tomatoes,
wild caught crustaceans, and prayed over turkey bacon.
Yup I be frontin in the midst of my survin...
Casing grocery store lines checkin for nosey friends n foes.
See I ain't supposed to be here...all educated with hands all
        adorned
with government handouts and paraphernalia.

See Tyrone use to call my phone, gettin all familiar.
Well, let's just say, he put me in away...and ahh, I let him slip in
        twins.
Now he doesn't call or come around much-
Useta   carry shame n such, because he didn't stake claims
or care to share his last name...now I'm a baby mama forced into
        drama.

Yup, I be frontin in the midst of my survivin...
Learned quickly to calculate, reduce and divide embarrassments...
Ensuring less eyeball rollins n sighs   and teeth smackins, with
        the cashiers
during WIC transactions.

By mentally adding and converting all the ounces to pounds
while thinking this system is profound –
Knowing some of these twisted frowned mouths
stands on the same ground.
Like mine their postures are bent, spent bobbin n weaving n being
looked on as a crook.

But, I keep a smile though, once in a while, I step my feet in the
        doors
in the arounda-way mom n pop stores.
To greet my real reality with sweet tasting civility…and to
        bargain for sweet cereal
and more.

Verses Sitting Dormant

I'm without
a plethora of vocabulary...
but my appetite is ridiculous, indefinable yet refined. ....
My footprints mystify most...it looks like encrypted codes
        belonging to unknown
worlds.
Although, in my opinion I swear I left this one a few times....
My mouth houses infinite chapters of unspoken words screamin
        to speak...
The revolution I seek
has yet to come... so volumes of freedom verses sit dormant
        behind
my teeth and gums.

I See You...

I see you, I see you
and I know who you are,
as the rest of the world refuses to.
I see you standing powerful
as the sun n stars,
as those   near and far
rejects the energy you are.
I see you, I see you
your connections to the universe.
It's unfathomable that anyone could
disgrace and misplace   your worth
your origin   your swagger...
then deny you as the world's *first-f*ather
being honorable   knowledgeable   royal   a king.
See It's plainly evident
in your divine vibe   your stride
your mean lean   in your
kinesthetic relations and vibrations
between your toes and feet   and
the earth's soil and   concrete.
See   I see you   I see you
and I know who you are
I know who you are
as the power "that be"
evil and its evil spawn, stand in envy
appalled   confused   mad
with greed n grandeur vision
not long   marriages with illusions of
supremacy was conceived-born.

Growing up and out
weaving webs of mass destruction n hate.
Exhausting all vigor, vigorously
by studying you-your beat
endlessly...
See they confiscated you
your aesthetics
but couldn't figure
then unapologetically defined you
a useless nigger.
The cognitive dissonance
double crossed crucifix
God-like complex
all works best for them.
He who defines   rules.
But still I see you
and I know who you are
as the rest of the world refuses to.
I won't be mystified
as you completely defy
and redefine the rules.
reconnect ties
disclaim their names and lies
and rise.
See my eyes are loyal
it's born out of the same soul,
made of the same soil.
See   I see you, I see you
your reserved mystique
posturing inside
and around your physique
as it radiates a profound shine
to your crown   limbs   and feet.
Mirroring your inner royalty
your Moorish ancestry   your kin.

Even though you have forgotten.
The deep within was pushed too far
But I won't forsake you
because you picked up
the guns and bacon.
Started self-hatin n abandonin your families,
callin on false deities.
But In the midst of it all
I evaluate, never hated   relate   judged all.
I know you've
yet to receive the total recall
or awakened.
See they Frankensteined you,
nigger reframed you, renamed you
arrested developments in you,
commoditized you   noted you a fool
rewrote history in school as a tool
claimed it a mystery,
fed it to you like it was
honey and bread.   You fed.
All is not dead
I see you burning several holes
in them old Massa beds.
that's why they keep
watchin n killin ya
its paranoia and   xenophobia
See   I see you, I see you
You are pieces of my whole
a resilient soul
the one loved by the sun
created first on earth
my beautiful brilliant
divine Blackmoor brother
my shine   my armor.

Selling Hurt

Cashier lady rested her hand
in mine   her finger tips to my palm
divine like   all knowing   solemn.
She said   "can I help you"? Can I   help you?
My soul stood up   throbbed   and made eyes   with questions…
started self-dialoguing with itself folding into itself.
Do I lay down my surrender flag?   My help wanted signs?
Is it that evident?   Can you repeat the question?
Maybe she was just doing her job   I couldn't decode…
what was being exchanged or sold.
Can she really see   through my shirt?   My heart?
These pounds and pounds of hurt?

Freestyle Meetings

I've yet to meet every part of myself. Haven't greeted every language spoken, or felt all earths' soils between my toes. But heaven knows, once awoken n exposed, mingled n met, my single actions are unmet, thoughts thickened. I come for it all, no-holds-barred. I'm climbing up through nostrils, pushing noses wide open, sliding freestyle down tonsils, adding soul food   to life's gut. Consequently, I have to excuse all misunderstandings in such. Thus, my moves are confusing to the untrained eye, but mesmerizing and appreciated by those that rock shades to protect their third eye...

Blue Black and Brown Beautiful

Blue Black and Brown ladies and girls are beautiful, simply
        beautiful.
Skin tones the epitome of earth tones… burnish red and brown
        clay deep down in
the earth   beautiful   to fertile soil rich in fruits and oil
        beautiful.
To vintage colored tan sand beaches   beautiful.
Blue Black and Brown ladies and girls are beautiful, simply
        beautiful.
Nina Simone playing endlessly   on keys   wood from ebony
        trees
in-between authentic ivory   on a Mahogany piano   polished up
        shiny   beautiful.
Midnight blue black lit New York skyline   beautiful.
Black patent leather Mary Jane shoes, worn to grandmas
on Sundays and birthdays   beautiful
Little brown boys and girls   beating heat   splashing their feet
        in the street
making memories on hot black tar and concrete   in open fire
        hydrant
forgetting where they are   beautiful.
Panthers from the wild with sleek fur coats   with a powerful
        core and command
to the Black Panther Party   from Oakland   with black berets
        afros   leather coats
powerful core and command   beautiful.
Blue Black pregnant women with shinny skin   walking and
        singing alongside the
Blue Nile   beautiful.
Blue Black and Brown ladies and girls are beautiful, simply
        beautiful.
Dozens upon dozens of fresh tapped boiled down maple syrup
        filled in mason jars
beautiful

Mom's bear hugs and honey coated kisses   beautiful.
Dark chocolate morsels melting in Lil Brown princesses
easy bake ovens   Beautiful.
Brown skins of Jamaican grown coconuts   beautiful.
Creamy oatmeal   with   raw sugar and cinnamon sticks   stirred
          in   black cast
iron pots   on a cold winter morning   beautiful.
Blue Black and Brown ladies and girls are beautiful, simply
          beautiful.
Blue Black and Brown ladies and girls are beautiful, simply
          beautiful.
Blue Black and Brown ladies and girls are beautiful, simply
          beautiful.
Blue Black and Brown ladies and girls are beautiful, simply
          beautiful.
Blue Black and Brown ladies and girls are beautiful, simply
          beautiful.

Beautiful She

You
You are beautiful
I am beautiful
You
You are beautiful
I am beautiful
You
You are beautiful
I am beautiful
You
You are beautiful
I am beautiful
You
You are beautiful
I am beautiful
You
You are beautiful
I am beautiful
You
You are beautiful
I am beautiful
You
You are beautiful
I am beautiful
You
You are beautiful
I am beautiful
You
You are beautiful
I am beautiful

Walked

Walked with my
spiritual Sister
talked in real time
spontaneity chimed
so together   we
picked   wild
dark raspberries
entertained familiar spaces
never minded all time
Dined at the finest hour...
dates and cool water
were thee   divine   devour

Alhamduliallah

Colorful She

Her movements are colorful   spontaneous
Unapologetic like grandma's red painted toes or 4 inch red
        stilettos,
and fields of powerful yellows   beautified by bodacious
        ornamentals.
Like sighted green hues   of African royal jewels   and diamonds
        without conflicts.
Powerful like the purple chakara that connects the soul   to the
        cosmic.
Like rhythmic blues and indigos break dancing through windows
        in the morning
awakening anew   paralleling colors stretched over oceans   and
        skylines
after a regale   of doves   crying.

Permanent Recesses

Tiny open spaces created crumbly walls
within and away from her normalcy
building holes and vacuums.
overtime recesses in her projection
curved her time   spine and mind
permanently and completely out of line
fading light   dimming purpose.

She tried some time ago…way back then
to refashion her mode   what looked like a side show
to patch   to fill and refill her holes
her wounds   her feelings
to remove   herself from shading   her own light.

Her fight and try   is gone now.   It went on   to long.
She done stopped looking for her shadow.
Light and knowhow is needed   she told herself
understanding it is something she cannot buy
or find on a shelf or with someone else.
No hyperboles   only evidence of let go's
slow seductive dances in the dark
with pain   with complacency.
It was a spectacle to see
how it all went from hard   to easy.

Unsettling

Can't settle you down
like dust cascading over white sheets
on forgotten furniture pieces

Fussed over
fooling myself
- to sleep
- too gather myself

by stuffing memories of you
delicately Into
an antique
cedar hope chests

My Young Lady in Waiting

A moment of silence for my 16 year old daughter was
all days   in a day.
A day to fuss over her hair and makeup   and dress.
She was always so picky about clothes and her eyebrows
So I knew I needed a team   some royal assistance.
She was a princess after all   getting prepared for an audience
a young lady in waiting   to see the one true king.
The ladies of our family acted as her personal ladies maids.
Dressed her up in a white gown and white flowered crown.
The jewels was easy   I always knew she would wear
my wedding day pearls on her special day
while resting my proud eyes upon her   telling her she did well.

Just never thought it would be this day   in a moment of silence.

A Moment of Silence (part 1)

A moment of silence mean
family   aunties   God mommies
and sand box friends   fly across the sky
take that drive   shows up   steps up.
Empathize.   Sympathize.
Brings peace   becomes ah mouthpiece
make blankets   write reflections   set the table
drink tea and honey   turn sad to funny.
Cancel plans.   Do all they can.
Skip work. Call out sick. Grows d- -ks.
Cook food.   Answer the calls
Fuck all.

It is someone's baby's last show. Mine!

A Moment of Silence (part 2)

A moment of silence mean
a lot of me died inside.
Praying long.   Holding on.
Not sweating the small.
Staying up late.   Rejecting trivial calls.
Falling.   Standing up.
Longing about time.
Feeling capable of walking away
from all things   and into everything.
Being afraid of quiet spaces.
Wishing for do overs and reruns….
Working daily to be sound   stay around.
Crying all-night long   staying strong
Faking grins, holding it in for my other children,
otherwise being ready to pass on.

It was my baby's last show.

A Moment of Silence (part 3)

A moment of silence mean
shut your face.
Respect space.
Pray.
Put yo egos away.
Ignore all side shows.

It is someone's baby last show. **Mine.**

A moment of silence mean
shut your face.
Respect space.
Pray.
Put yo egos away.
Ignore all side shows.

It is someone's baby last show. **Mine.**

Woman to Woman

Release all those bags
listen to the lady
name
Conscience
that sits heavily on your shoulders
ranting and raving
about your needs.

Shake off the past damages…
Inhale new possibilities…
Reach around
to the nape of your neck,
grab your spine
and pull it up

Watch-out
faithfully
for everything will
fall into
place…

A Rose

A rose I was called
I couldn't be
can't afford
the liabilities
thorns never tickled me
I rather be a dandelion
a flower by my definition
it grows around
rusted metal and stockade fences
stop signs lifeless rocks-
and organic ornamental gardens
decreeing its belonging

I Gave

(For Gabby Douglas, 2012 and 2016 U.S. Olympics Gymnast and champion)

I gave   I gave   I gave
I gave   my arch   my curves   my sweat   my bends
my air my twist my tears my pose
my jumps   my fears   my posture   my fall
my pain my dance my swing my all
my stretch my curl my swirl my form my strike
my shakes my leaps my hope my fight
my nerves my poise my thrust my fuss
my real my time my grind
my front my stage my page
my stare my brow my black my cool
my slack   my inner   my hip my flip
my reach my sass   my girl
my soul my goal my dream my style my swag my bags
my natural   my out my heart my wonder
my space my thunder my pout
my grin my gold my silver my best   my bad my win
my gut my strut   my care my share
my edge my stay my brave my last
my rare   my cry my try my bouts
my glory my story my cheer my shouts
my trust my happy my game my name
Gabby Douglas
sadly
my hair my hair my hair my hair   my hair   claimed
my enslaved sistah's and brotha's focus.

Everything

At the same time I met him
I met fine, alright, and loudness,
even haughty and I don't give damn.

He was my cigarettes after coffee,
my morning news, hangovers,
my rhythm and blues...
he was everything crooked and straight.

When a Purse Becomes a Bag

Back when my shoulders were small, and thin,
my armpit choked a trendy Fendi little red purse.
feather- light   swingin   with every jerk and turn,   not yet
         learned.
O-h the days of nothingness   one zippered compartment   depth
         was shallow…

Then   promises of spring time had come   and gone   over
         and over.

Little red Fendi purse   gracefully bows   carried plunged into
         maturity.
Now, not only bears lip-gloss   but tissues for the unexpected
         issues.
Realism done crept in   holding hands   strong with the *alarm
         clock*,
Started to wake up   a heavier make-up   carrying around quality
         in my time   world events
Keys to unseen doors   returns on receipts   my own pain killer n
         pacifiers   mom jeans
goals n dreams, self-esteem   skepticisms   being shook
         free will, bills and check books

While fictive kin sisters'   mommies' and aunties' spoke on
         trying to save us
Angela Davis   Bell Hooks   Shirley Chisolm   Lauryn Hill
         Assata Shakur
Sharazad Ali   Nina Simone   Sister Souljah   Francis Cress
         Welsing   Gwendolyn Brooks
profile photos   sittin on thrones   lookin the same look
brows high   lips pressed   eyes glazed ova   as to say "I told ya"
thicker   fuller shoulders   needs a bag.

Same Man

Sister I hear your heart through one
we hold dear in common...
For the sake of Allah
A mans heartbeat that holds weight
Immeasurably.   Uncommon.
But it is Allah the merciful
the most great that operates   holds power...

By only Allah's permission our brother
gives light in our connection.
For that my sister he is protected and blessed
as all our deen and family grows   flower.
Thus, spiritually we have mirrored desires...

I make dua
for you & he habitually
and believe you do the same for me.
Clearly Allah knows best
what's in our heart and our make...
It is he we cannot fake.
My dear sister please know
the benefits outweighs
any and all test
insha'Allah

Momma Morning Saga

Minutes into the blue-gray light
of morning
"Ma can you" "Ma where is-
"Ma"-" Maaaaa"…
Water fights ferociously
with every bowl-n enamel in sight
Rhythmically and
unsympathetically feet drum
each stair
Doors chairs
cabinets, countertops and cups
all screams what the
Stolen sip sounds quietly
escapes out
As coffee ceremoniously lines
my throat
alongside questions and threats-
both grizzly and melodiously
spoked.
The "do you have(s)" ?
The "you better not misses"
The "you ain't too big"
side eyes   and kisses…

Fireflies

My present nowadays reaches back into my familiar; secretly masturbating time…today I'm in the arena with swollen tits, assault rifles, riding on the backs of fireflies… callus calves cry for stilettos and forward moving time … as I try to be present, in my own presence…the clichés, the upheavals, the disturbances, even the fruits and blessings all reaches back into my familiar masturbating time.

tell me wouldn't it be great just to catch fireflies?

Denied in Writing

I write because
my heart is broken.
The same time
my eyes saw something
beautiful;
unreachable in reach
denied the try
swaddle by a hand
when I caressed the smoothness
of my man's warm thigh
I am writing out my cry

Lie

Our fukn everthing.
is fukn nothing?
F u c k i n g   NOTHING ?
Fukn to fuck ? WHAT?
FUCK   YOU   you fucking lie !
You   Fuckin Lie!
You lied...
to my-my everything.
You lied   to my toes, my thighs,
MY EYES   My-my mind and time.
You fucking   lied.
As you fluidly
freely   touched me
penetrated me   sucked me   tasted me...
Wined and dined me
promised to   love me
you fukn lied.
FUCK   YOU   and
Fuck your   mishandlings'
Fuck your watch   your talks
on bad time and timings-
you   are   lying
f u c king lying.

Free Me

free me
over the
reoffending
endings ending me

Free me over
the fading
the findings
now shelved in me

free me over
the gatherings
prevailing me
from being…

Residue

You stuck to me like posted notes.
Memories and choices made
cannot be unglued ...
The residue and goo is to thick.
Now, I have mental notes
on how not to deal with you.
You read me
well and wrote me off
in your notebook,
filed me away as a project,
one of your female contradiction.
Knowing full well I don't deserve your tricks.
None of your interest
are in line with   your interest.
your new name is   master of confusion.
Don't no if you know it or not   my friend
you are indeed a pirate
that steals hearts and crush spirits
and make women physically sick
and mentally screwed...

You are a   hypocrite...and a liar...think
you should become a cult leader
lord knows you are the greatest deceiver.

your best friend warned me...
guess I didn't want to believe it
no need for a prediction. That would suggest
that my father raised a full out fool.
You add to the list of men that women
learn to hate.
While you sit there with the devils grin.
You will end up having nothing in the end.
I must give it to you my brother

you had me pull from deep within
your grand accomplishment was getting yours off...
on my weakness.
You killed my joy
now I am thinking all men are out to destroy.

Black Bird Fly

Black bird fly
turn your
pupils away
from mine
go on   fly

my   spine is
reconnecting

stop shapeshifting

Fly   Fly
leave me
and my
side eye alone

your wings
aren't friends
to my
rib bone sides
Fly

Who?

Whose' hair are you
pullin
Whose pussy are you
licken
body flipin
whose back are you
arching
thighs' n legs
are you   quivering –
sqeezin'
Who are you
pleasing
readin'
Who's getting
Part of It all
making the fall
of my tears
seem law
my nerve endings
crawl?
Tell me
whose gettin'
my call?

Ah Piece

Can a sistah get ah piece
I've done repurposed last night
chicken bones twice
nuttin but   nuttin
but soup, beans and rice.
I heard freedom iz absolute
So I went back to school.
The professors were cool.
Still can't seem to get my
subjects and verbs right.
Done got pimped and a *B.S.* diploma.
Now lookn in da mirror   all it be I see
is a server   servin..
See Summa   mother freakn cum laude
aint feedin me.
Paid my-my everthing and all my money.
I just wanna know   can ah Sistah
get ah piece?

I be hungry…

A Divorcée Testimony

When you know when it's time to go.
When eyes look into time not into eyes.
When conversations becomes a   remember when.
When love makin   loses its catharsis   and the kisses.

Grandma's Dust Pan

Standing in grandmas broom closet
the last place left to look.
Mental notebook readied
for answers I came to find.
Finished searching through
the kitchen pantry,
drawers and cabinets
flipped through all the dulled ice picks,
bruised fruits,   junk drawers and more   twice over.
raided both linen and bedroom closets
strapless bags, shoe boxes with sole-less shoes
in the hunt for her   dissimilar and similar trials
unwanted burdens…and rectifying solutions
questioning her hiding and learning places…
just to understand my open convoluted spaces.
To deal with and hide mine…to be alright, even fine.

Who Letcha Out

Ya make a
sistah get
all Indignant
wanna summon
all ya lineage
give thanks
n congrats to ya
mother   father
in all ya kin
then ask them
who letcha ya out
the door...?
who letcha in?
Ya do to much
are to much.
Ya disturb
and make
peace and such
employ a sistah
to move things
touch things
become undone.
Track miles
create mounds
move mountains
surf clouds
pray for showers
think for hours
pour out oceans
control emotions
seed the earth
check her worth
claim time
get in line

loose fear
breathe up
the same
free air.

I Ain't

The hole in the mattress
I ain't   Damn you
I gave you my life
The home for low grade insults
I ain't   Damn you
I gave you my life
The fires for your silky haired desires
I ain't   Damn you
I gave you my life
The Desperate Housewife
I ain't   Damn you
I gave you my life
Damn you   Damn you
I gave you my life.

Living Poetry (part 1)

Living poetry happens while I'm sleep and I awaken because of your stare. It happens when I still feel the impression of your warm mouth on my forehead after you have gone to work. When you tease me about my fears and quirks, or morning honking and snorts. When I'm cooking or you are cooking and I want more pepper and you want more salt. It happens at night when I bite my bottom lip, as you grip my hips, bracing, gyrating, uncontrollably shaking…to quiet my moans while caught up in love throws…sometimes I call you daddy and you say oh, oh shit honey, and we stop because we have awakened the baby.

Being Natural

Naturally my unnatural comfort your natural fears
How unnatural it'll be for me to aide & abet you, to compromise me,
Imprison my *free to be*   to comfort you...
Fear on naturally as you do, this natural Sistah shun
The unnatural...naturally.

Forward Moving

Forward walking
through nature's
natural journey
roots, leaves
branches & fall
transitions and truths
with no curves
or brush fires...
Nestled between
the edge of changes
and the river flows
loosening tattered memory
and embracing
all the let go's
Emancipating ill dysfunction
disowning meaningless names
all second handed
unchanging emotions
constancy versus constancy...
Striving to revert
placing limitless value
on divinity, faith and moral desires...
causing the inner Roman antics to retire

A Sistah Riding for Her Brothers Lady

Pockets

Agreeably I rode
my ass in ya   left back pocket.
The crushed mahogany
leather wallet occupied the right one.
Pocket trims burned the copper tones   of my arms,
as I hung out to catch rear views.
Shoutin' Hotep Hotep   and givin salaams
to ma Sistahs n ma Brothers…
Afro flowin   big   fresh n raw
barefoot and all   dangling around
like wild little monkeys   swinging upside-down in trees.
Time to time comfortably   with confidence
you took the solo honor   to align our views n flow
so   in peace   I rested my head and feet
on the two lint piles   settled in ya pocket   corners.

Single Momma Lady

A Boy Needs

A boy needs his father,
not when it's convenient,
not just when ya feel like
being bothered
A boy needs his father
and not just in-between
ya   Ms. New Thing

Lady to Lady

You've done put me in a fix   done added a suffix
to my husband's last name. Thought it be me
givin him his 1st son. Yes, I'm all in my feelings
my heart is broken. But here's a token.
If I may be so bold   to share what I refuse
being sold, some time ago…
Anotha said she too   was swept up by his
promises and his kisses. He assured her
he'd leave my bed. He did.   Not for her
but for she and she and yes   even she…
I know you might   misunderstand me.
I'm just trying to speak   lady to lady
as she too   was trying to speak to me.
I'm warning you   as she warned me.
But I see he have you   as he had me.
Fixed on pipe dreams, material things…anything
but the metaphysical and logical… forgetting who I am
like a lost art. Even thought   I had special parts
to change his heart. Sorry to say Ms. Lady   there's no such
          thing as
special parts...It's about the right foundation from the start.

Air of Self-Faith

As the cloud thickens
shading clarity intermittently
mirroring my reality
my throat arches frequently
bending and pulling to make room for air
My life endeavors-upheavals   moves
floating   darkening
with & without cordiality.
Uninvited - decidedly *convolution* and *chance*
lows & plateaus mingled & mingles with
my sanity and nerve endings
conditioning my centered morality – modalities.
Consequently, the east faced bottle closed mouth opens
and captures the eastern rain.

Inspired by Surah Baqarah   2:153, 2:155 & 2:15

Loss Wombs

Wombs' releasing newborns
without knowing of its wounded wombs
baring unknown shortfalls, hunger and Ideals
ears of the mute - unseeing eyes, sewn lips, forgotten tongue
just alive with aborted souls...taking up air
leaving full-grown newborns trying to reborn itself.

Folks and Their Daughters

Folks rather see their daughters well-traveled, ran through like
        whores…getting
venereal sores.
Folks rather see their daughters experimenting and playing pet the
        kitty,
with other kitties.
Folks rather see their daughters have four or more boyz or men
Humping their daughters   like dogs in backseats of cars   having
        fits when called
a Bitch… learning hard lessons and being ditched.
Folks rather see their daughters shacked up, living with a baby
daddy   being a baby momma and a single lady with her hands up.
instead of a married lady, passing on generational messages
        about the right way
of passage. Folks rather see their daughters make the same
        mistakes.
Because they can't see young marriages as a moment to
        celebrate…
it's treated like a great debate…not as relaxed as when daughters
        come in
late from a date…can't even walk straight.
Young marriages, family building, communal living
are not seen or tried as a contribution or solution, to a possible
        start of a
revolution...something to build on or make good on…
to right the wrong… It is seen as a guaranteed fail,
a mistake…something to frown upon and hate on…
Folks rather see their daughters wedded and controlled by Uncle
        Sam…
Set up with the ultimate disenfranchised family plan whereas the
        woman
has to kick out the man and become the woman and the man.

Still Standing

There was a lady left to fin and fight.
Left to figure it out. She was a beautiful chocolate thing.
Judging folks calls her a black thing, bad things.
Based on knowing some obvious things…
Can she be a flower? Get a flower?
She loved hard   aged hard. Perhaps carelessly and desperately
      too.
Between her surviving, coping, self-medicating, yearning, tiring,
      abusing.
giving, trying, losing, rebounding, falling, fighting, caring and not
      caring.
Oh she entertained horrible things, wild things. She lost things.
      Everything.
One would say she lost it in her early teens…She would tell you
      she lost it at three.
Sadly she had nobody telling that part of her story or how she
      became to be.
Walking a mile in her shoes   one might have to congratulate her
      for standing…and some respect too.

A Sister Keeper Mission

Sisters
we must
invest in   us.
celebrate the day
when we do not say
how much
or what for.
Sisters we need to
give more,
later for the
tunnel vision
of spending
tens N   twenties
shaking our booties,
seeking fruitless
salvation
in the clubs
perspiring.
Sweatin   the   why?
Mr. or Brotha
Stay frontin
never tryin
to give his time
then marries anotha
after you gave up   the grind.
We wonder why
So many are
expiring or despising
and questioning
why our community
is so torn   disenfranchised.
Come on spend time
even hours   spreading dawah.
Let's help each other

handle foul claims
that claims nothin
in return for our attention
or tomorrow's redemption.
not to get all grimy or rhymy
but sisters we need
to look to the top
and stop   paying
trying to be slayed
getting inked up in pink
renaming ourselves   Barbies
showing our butts
and for "WHAT" ?
like Nikki Minaj ?
Save to make hajj
Learn about the
Isra and Mi'raj
Re-think the
Individual usual paths.
Enlist Into anew
Sisterhood army
a divinely protected journey
to resurrect the dead...
of the femininity entity,
to forsake the feminist make.
Break bread with me
stay up late with me
plotting, reenergizing
how to make
our lives great.
For heaven sake
I am hungry
Sing me a song
call the Adan
extend the door
I implore   you
to expect more
to Invite me in,
to submit more
bend with me

put our heads
to the floor
Come on…
help me
fight my best
against the whispers
and test
nourish my intellect
help me keep
my heart   from   going dark.
We can't afford
to be hypocritical
backbiting sisters
picking apart sisters.
we all had ill starts.
what the hell
it's only a fail
labeling "her"
a jezebel
explain what's
not for sale.
Choose humility
Scale down
the judgmental views
and the
"I'm better then you"
mentality.
In reality
all sisters imans faced calamities.
As believers   sister keeper
revolutionary designers
share the proper lessons
and revere
Allah's blessings

The *Every Kinda Lady* Short Stories

Author's Notes

Disabilities aren't always visible and people aren't always sympathetic. I dedicate this to my daughter and to parents and caregivers who have a child with chronic health issues, special needs, or physical or mental disabilities. In addition, I hope if teachers, caretakers, and extended family members read this please do some reflection and note how valuable and influential and even harmful your actions can be.

"She Stares Out the Window" includes the poem "God Why My Flower Child." "She Stares Out the Window" is a short powerful story about the strength and faith of a mother and child faced with chronic health conditions. The world can be such a cold and unaccommodating and insensitive place for children faced with challenges that could scar them emotionally and socially for the rest of their life…as well as a beautiful place with at least one patient advocate or support system.

She Stares Out the Window

She stares out the window grinning with her nose, forehead, and chin pressing against the warm dated school windows. Elbows ashen from the window ledge rubbings, she is bobbing and weaving as she pretends the kids are playing tag with her. "You missed me" she utters. She traces the arches of the rusted red swing with her eyes as she synchronizes her inhaling's and exhaling's rhythmically with the ups and downs and the back and forth of her friends swinging. She holds tightly onto the waxy fat green Crayola crayon because letting go would somehow tamper with her reality. Coloring for her has never become a fair trade off. But the crayons have become loyal friends, never leaving her indoors, alone. The green crayon with its tattered wrapper and spotted exterior from being over used and fused with others is her favorite.

The artist uses all the other colors in the box to fill up the white pages in her notebook. For she notices the papers need her; the papers are deprived of many colors; a canvas without pleasures or stories to share with others. The fragile young artist sits short of content, drawing school houses with flowers and rainbows. She always starts her ventures with the color green. The green Crayola crayon has powers the other crayons do not. For her the green crayon is capable of opening and terminating the drawings. The green crayon covers the earth, hiding the dirt she never includes in her pictures. Without failure, ceremoniously, her right hand cradles the immanent friend, the green crayon, and rigorously scribbles all over the colorful flowers and rainbows.

Recess is over and the day is ending. Knia tucks her crayons away exhaling some hopeless energy. She is now somewhat content as her cheeks are rising high, smiling wide showing all her teeth except for the front top two; for those fell out her mouth months ago. Thus, she knows the day is ending, not because she can tell time, but because of the routine scheduled events. The teacher writes on the blackboard, reminding the class to bring in their 100TH day projects for the 100th day parade, and recess will be canceled for our special visitor. An emotion without form or familiar arises in Knia; she is overjoyed, at school. Knia kneels down, softly pressing her lips closely to the opening of the desk, whispering good- bye to her green crayon friend, telling it that she won't be seeing it tomorrow...

The 100th day of kindergarten, rivals the first days of school for millions of light-hearted, eager 5year olds. Pennies, pasta, beads, and Legos and other tiny meaningless, assessable things are strung, marinated and manipulated in Elmer's glue, then paraded around elementary schools like trophies, telling the spectators there is nothing to debate, thus proudly memorializing the 100th day of school is their right.

The day is winding down, and the sun has gone into hiding...

Knia says, "Mommy will you be you coming to my 100th day of school tomorrow? I want you to see the parade". And...and...and the teacher is giving out prizes "and" "and" Count Dracula from Sesame Street is coming to help us count to one Hundred...and...and ...and..."

Mom says "hey, hey honey slow down, I know you can't wait for tomorrow, I am happy for you. Sorry my sweet flower but I cannot come to the parade tomorrow; but I just might make it there by the end of the day. Now, now, say your prayers and ask Allah to increase your faith, because sometime it's the first thing we lose, because..."

"I know ma," Knia interrupts, "we cannot see it or touch it, and you just have to believe!"

"Good night sweetie!" her mom says.

Knia's, excitement lingered throughout the night, capturing and shortening her hours of sleep. Finally the morning's hustle and bustle greeted them with the same replays...the lets go's', the come ons'- eat ups-don't miss your buses'- hugs, kisses 'and enjoy your days'.

"Good morning class" the teacher says.

The Student's says "good-morning Ms.SlaChov."

The teacher stands in front of the class and announces that today is the 100th day of school, delivering a message the children already know is coming; about the parade and special visitor. Shifting in their seats and feet tapping sounds are suspending in the air. The air is thick with fresh innocents and anticipation, giving patience a cause to retire. Knia raises her hand asking to share her project. "Not now Knia," Ms.SlaChov says, rolling her eyes. Sighing, as she always does when dealing with Knia. "However, I need to make an announcement that I'm sure all of you are going to favor." Ms.SlaChov continues, instead of completely missing recess I decided we will skip mourning work centers and go outside." Ms.SlaChov's, words continue serenading their ears like the chiming sounds of the ice-cream truck.

Knia's ears; however, are not hearing the same tones. Her throat arches and a salty tear rolls down her face. Knia's, medical condition and the cold weather for the last two weeks have worn her downhearted. Knia's spirit is silencing itself minute by minute as the teacher continues talking. She only hears muffling sounds, like glass breaking under water. Ms.SlaChov drags her old penny loafers slowly and unsympathetically over to Knia, placing Knia's coloring notebook on her desk. "Stop that crying and take out your crayons. Blame it on your parents and laws of eugenics, it not my fault you have to stay inside...

Knia, takes out her crayons as instructed, as the rest of the class is running outdoors laughing, clowning and screaming "tag your it"... Knia, just sits limp, losing her will, this time she does not grab for her best friend, the green fat Crayola crayon; she grabs the brown crayon, drawing herself laying down and then grabs the green crayon and proceeds to draw grass on top. But just then Knia's mom walks in quietly hoping to surprise her. Mom sees the image of death, her flower child is drawing and says to her daughter "You have to keep your faith", "you have to believe for both of us" in a voice as strong as a broken mother could.

God Why My Flower Child

As spring time shits out
Repeats   out
nature's sweet sweet newborns
I question   she questions   Doctor Try These question
As the rich
the famous
tear ducts release common salty tears of the poor
Lily, Rose, Iris and Black Eyed Suzy wilted petals desire fall
and   no more
I question   She questions   Doctor Try These question
as all the right brains questions the left
When opportunity gives chance for us to spring a smile
my heart bleeds out
my soul repeats out
ephemeral   no more
My mouth is weary filled with glass and cotton
As spring time shits out
repeats out
nature's sweet- sweet newborns
Flower's heavy eyes ask why
as I question
Why do my offspring suffer?

The first sound and the last sound of my daughter's heartbeat will stay with me forever…She spoke to me through her heartbeat literally.

Knia Khaye Hutchings 7/12/2000 – 5/8/2017

Dedication

"The Fixed Honey Brown Lady on the Perm Box" is dedicated to all the little dark skin and natural girls in the world who were made to feel ugly, imperfect or broken? Please know you are not. "The Fixed Honey Brown Lady on the Perm Box" includes the poems "Black like Me?" and "Our Story Version 2." When hate and negative self-image issues are not realized, but fostered, handed down and grossly unintentionally shared...The love of self and self-image becomes an arduous journey, whereas the traveler tends to travel the scenic route, like a tourist going sightseeing, to view or experience something never seen. Hate in this manner is handed out, forced in internally, coming from something unnatural, evil, ignorant, opposing and external. Only a few will ever realize and escape the saga or miss the handouts.

The Fixed Honey Brown Lady on the Perm Box

[**Mother**] Oh sugar shack, aww sulky, sulky now, well isn't that something? Shoot ha, ha! I just burnt my tongue. Can't believe what I just read Fatima.

[**Fatima**] Alright, ma what are you over there reading that got you spilling coffee all over your white linen table cloth?

[**Mother**] Well, this USA Today an article written by Michelle Healy states that 36% of African American women are wearing their hair natural 10% more since 2010, and predicts that at least in 2012 it will jump another 10% putting women who wear what Allah has given them naturally in the majority. Fatima, this means folks are going nappy-happy. Black women are giving up the creamy crack.

[**Fatima**] So what!

[**Mother**] So what? Honey see you're wearing braids right now, back in the days it was frowned upon when black women wore braids to work; it was consider un-professional, plenty women was fired. Don't believe me google Rogers vs. American Airlines.

This reminds me when I got my first perm and how I loved being with aunt BD, your great aunt Big Dee. Back when I was young and naive I cherished all compliments I received from aunt Big Dee. Aunty Big Dee never failed to say to me that I was a pretty black girl, or that I was special because I was cute to be so dark. My aunt was my favorite person, besides my dad. As a preteen I nicked named myself brownie, because brownies were my favorite chocolate dessert and it was dark like me.

[**Fatima**] "You mean it still is your favorite, you just inhaled three pieces.

[**Mother**] Hush now, let me tell you...
Because Big Dee is my father's oldest sister she did everything. When I was small, my cousins and I called aunty Big Dee because

she was very tall, for short we called her BD. Aunty BD, spent many weekends with me showing me all the different corners of the world. One weekend I remember she picked me up. I couldn't wait; I remember thinking the five days that came before Friday was going by slowly, on purpose like. Aunty Big Dee said this weekend was going to be the best weekend ever. This weekend she said will be overflowing with big girl kind of stuff. I just knew the surprise had to be she was going to bring me to buy my first training bra, a white bra the kind with the tiny pink bow on the front. However, she brought me to another elegant restaurant. The restaurants that served food on white oversize plates, tables covered with white linen, several utensils and serious looking people, whom seemed to never have conversations.

BD would order food for both of us, giving me no options. "No, you may not have a choice" sat heavily in her crow's feet, flared nostrils, and tight mystified smile. I was not disappointed; I remember viewing her as an expert, well-informed about fancy stuffy restaurants and cafés with white linen table cloths and such. I figured I might even order the wrong thing, something common. Consequently, I obeyed my aunt's deep alto, protective, yet authoritative voice and demands. She would set the tone just before we walked in the restaurant saying things to me like "Remember" I better not have to remind you on how to behave". I swear the words bypassed her mouth straight to my face, ears, and chest from her gut, nearly smothering me. However, I did not care because I felt like she was introducing me to some fancy society. I justified her actions, thinking I too would be considered fancy, an expert. Everything she said was spot-on without error. Aunt BD, ended the affair with a one sided verbal interchange, a one sided discussion, by saying, "honey the money on the table belongs to the nice waitress; it's the proper thing to do"…I thought Aunty BD was also a mind reader; unless the window secrets in my eyes ratted me out. Her words alone always were the endings of our fancy meal conversations. Like a slice of sweet potato pie you earned after eating everything on you plate including the nasty black eyed peas and sticky gross pig feet.

Therefore, when she would tell me things like "you are cute to be dark", I believed her without paying any attention to the words *to be dark.* The word cute any other compliments immersed my shortcomings, wrapped me up, and lullabied my soul, fulfilling my needs from not having a mother around with a warm purple blanket, royal velvet cloak, a princess cloak of being. When my aunty Big Dee said those words to me I wished all three of my sisters were with me and my four brothers so they too could feel lullabied, warm, like royalty… I wondered why they all didn't share my daddy, we could of all stayed together. We all could've had fancy meals on white tablecloths. Well, no bra with the pink bow, but something just as rousing. Aunty BD was going to perm my thick hair. Discarding my afro puffs in exchange for straight ponytails fated to be rolled in pink sponge curlers. She told me she was fixing me up, although I never felt that my appearance was broken. My aunt convinced my father that my natural hair was out of style. Daddy ideals about taking care of my exterior and I.Q. were easy and satisfying like peanut butter and jelly without the crust.

Our Story
Daddy's rib bone sides
arms and armpits
cradled my small crown
Perfumed my braids
with Old Spice and Brut.
We Okayed each other
I recall mornings
when the sun awakenings,
rivaled the sleeping sun.
Dad executed his ideas
to take care of my
exterior and I Q.
He'd brushed   my locks,
100 strokes,
to unfold
my tight, curled hair,
we counted.
Our stories told tale
of dynamic duals,
perfecting the
imperfect

Well she fixed me alright. I can still hear aunt Big Dee's voice, just like it was yesterday bragging to her friends over the phone. I sat motionless with white creamy, smelly perm in my hair. I sat anxiously, eyes stretched waiting to see if my scalp was going to burn or tingle. I'd been warned that my hair could fall out if my scalp burned. I was warned not to scratch because it would burn and I was told to stay still so that the perm, the ammonia, kitty litter smelling, nose permeating chemicals, wouldn't get in my eyes and burn my eyeballs out.

I remember trying to imagine a bald me, I just couldn't fathom it. I recall asking Aunt BD if my eyebrows and eyelashes could fallout too. No! She said, obviously my curiosity offended her. Because, she hushed me up by yanking my head around. Then, I tried hard not to think about asking any more questions. I recall focusing my eyes on the perm box and the avocado green kitchen counter top, where the canisters and coffee maker were mingling with hair grease, combs and curlers and Meanwhile, BD she bragged to her friend about how she was prettying up her little niece by perming my hair. I could not wait to see the new me when it was done; because I was going to look like the honey brown lady on the perm box, the Dark in Lovely perm lady.

Later that evening my aunt's friends had intruded by coming over and interrupting things. Aunty Sandy and Aunty Red, I called them my aunts because that's the way family grown up friends wanted it. Aunt Red had red hair and light brown eyes and skin. I particularly paid attention to her because not many people looked like her. Without hesitation, BD's friends like annoying parrots, saying familiar words, "she is cute to be so dark, and she is a pretty black child." As if this were a public yet private meeting about my looks. As aunt Red- rubbed her hands through my hair and down my face, my moment of big smiles slowly synchronized downwardly with her hands. The tones in their voices seemed surprised and extra cheerful. I could feel my heart break, I could feel it tearing and bleeding. Although, I had treasured those words before, somehow coming out my aunt's friends' mouths they did not sound the same. I was offended, wounded, and awakened. I heard the other half of the phrase clearly, the mask was off. The words tangled upwards and downwards in my brain... to be so dark, to be so dark, and pretty to be so dark, dark. I began to think my fancy aunty BD, was cruel.

Why? I asked myself in my mind; why did my compliments from my aunt and her friends have a twist? As I sat giving a fake, half-parted smile as to say thank you, showing no disrespect, other questions crept into my mind. I was crying inside. Time stood still, hands on the clock moved slowly and unfavorably. The counters in the kitchen seemed bigger and the cabinet's knobs begun to look like eyes that pitied me. The plastic chair-cover wasn't bothering me anymore; I could no longer feel the bottom of my legs sticking to the seat. Suddenly, the weekend that I'd waited five long days for was too long. Could it be that normally dark-skinned girls were ugly? Did my aunt and her friends think there was something wrong with me?

Sadly, Fatima, I use to own those demeaning words, believed them and carried them around throughout my adolescent years. I hated being so dark. But my mother was so dark. I wanted nothing to do with so dark. I decided to hate aunt BD for her twisted compliments, for being careless with my feeling and disturbing my natural born peace. Nina Simone, the blues singer sang, *To be Young Gifted and Black* on my father's records almost daily. Did Nina mean lighter blacks? Daddy was as black as me. Maybe men don't mind being so black? Maybe black was a boyish color, daddy loved me, and so he had to love my kinda black…

Black Like Me

Was Nina Simone
Including black like me?
Black like me?
Black like me?
Where's my gifts?
My gifts?
My gift?
Am I too black for gifts?

———

I thought I was going to be mad at aunt BD forever, but time healed me. Growing, into my own person has helped. However, memories of my high school years at times still hurt my feelings. I felt that if I was just a few shades lighter I would look better. I think it's was because boys fell head over heels for girls they called "redbones". Television shows, music videos in the eighties and the nineties, almost always showcased lighter- skinned girls with long silky or weaved hair. I always had a head full of hair, long but it wasn't bone straight, limp, or silky naturally. The system of "White Supremacy" *con*-vinced us that light skin and straight hair are better and unfortunately a lot of dark skinned girls-young and old- were hurt by it. Acculturation, assimilation and transformation were the keys that were used to open the perm and bleaching cream locks that opened the door to the illusionary magical "white world" of acceptance and success.

The 60's ushered in a wave of Black pride, and slowly the consciousness of melanated people started to rise with phrases like, "the blacker the berry the sweeter the juice." Many folks began rejecting the organizations like the Jack and Jill Society that only allowed those that could pass the brown paper bag test. If you don't believe that you can look it up. The big girl me was not developed in my aunt's kitchen but through research, reading, spiritual awakening, introspection, maturation, understanding the negative influences of society, and family love.

It's who people are in the inside that determines beauty. It was a long journey coming to that realization. Call me radical if you want to, but I am proud of my skin tone, and I am perm free. That is one reason I wear my hair chemical free and natural. The other reason is, because I simply like it. I don't like the idea that being natural is unnatural, a fad, or out of style, and I definitely don't like running from the rain. I think the more people accept their natural selves the better their life and health will be-not to mention cheaper. I'm not judging people who decide to perm, color, or weave their hair. Just leave the babies alone, it leads to deep complexes, which are unnecessary. I just think it should be a choice-and not an indoctrination coming from a convoluted place. Children are not given the choice to see their natural beauty long enough, and before ya know it, someone comes along telling them they need fixin.

Original by Design

Chocolate   butter pecan   tan
Asiatic   blue   black hues.
Woolly soft fro   Kinky curly locs
styled in Harlem's tracks N blocs
crochet kotty knots ponytails   cornrows
smellin all   organic   like
coconut nd   Jamaican castor oil,
even blue magic N African royal.
Soul connecting window views
ranging from hazel brown
to midnight blues
ain't nottin but Allahs truths...
Natural feminine stance
dominant n swagger
Rhythm refinement is Prolific
poetically timed   intense .
Flawlessly complete,
carryin the original   woman   design
made by the divine   divinely
a Black girl she be
unapologetically

Trust, Truths & Love Quotes /Aphorisms

❖ Trust relinquishes suspicions . . . and gives birth to peace.

❖ My every nerve endings are moved by you...

❖ We all have quiet fires smoldering, looking for air to fan our flames...

❖ Wild fires have no form...Like emotions are without shape.

❖ Love and truths aren't made easy to put out of place...

❖ Truths-holds no sympathy, acquaintances, hands, or lies.

❖ Only men with an invested interest in women can begin to understand the inner workings of a lady.

❖ Daydreaming inwardly into the heart will tell you how brilliant and screwed up you are...

❖ Guardianship over true pleasures means one must comprehend and appreciate the images of life and death.

❖ Hard to believe those that bear untold stories don't have a witness.

❖ It's best to write the story before the storyline changes.

❖ I believe we all have butt naked coffee moments...

❖ Need post it notes on the bathroom mirror to remind me never to compromise my name.

❖ Compromised and convoluted what is the difference?

❖ The wild naturally plant seeds and craft spontaneous garden.

❖ Releasing bags allows for consciousness to move in.

❖ The best preparation is knowing...

- ❖ Freezing ones thought is as difficult as freezing time.

- ❖ Tomorrow mornings have the potential to be blissful…

- ❖ I can when I can…period end of story.

- ❖ When your voice is not your own you shouldn't speak

- ❖ Love and release are friends with truths and acceptance and profoundly understands rejections...

- ❖ Decided to cry a necessary cry today…Mourning a new beginning and ending.

- ❖ Changing our yesterdays is like knowing you will live tomorrow...you can't.

- ❖ How you live in your open and closed spaces, comes back to you in your open and closed spaces.

- ❖ Think all I might need is a good cry. The whole kicking and screaming kind. The out loud, I want my mommy and daddy kinda of cry. The kind that you start playing music and the song is all about you kinda cry. The kind whereas someone pats you on the back and say let it all out hun, let it all out, The kind when somebody say there's always tomorrow.

- ❖ Be proud of who you are wherever you are.

- ❖ There is enough sunshine for everyone.

- ❖ If you think it and want to write it…write it!

- ❖ Without pause, I know the greatest pain in life is losing a child.

Conversations with myself are the best…writing things out is like a personal Q&A session for me. I find it helps to organize my thoughts and avows my beliefs with clarity, although I am not always married to all my beliefs. Thus, I am growing and learning all the time. I often like to share my thoughts and ask questions to evoke thoughts and dialogue, so it is my thing, my trademark to include quotes, questions and sometimes photos at the end of work. Feel free to use the space below to express your thoughts and continue the conversation with others. I would love to be a part of the conversation…

If you would like to share your thoughts email me directly at **EveryKindaLady@gmail.com**.

Please note I welcome opposing viewpoints…

I don't know if all human beings on the planet have coined a word for the emotion we call "LOVE."

Perhaps some figured a word for some emotions are just tucked to deep, so profound, spread so wide open... that narrowing it down to a *word* to say is unnecessary...may even disturb, play down, undercut the emotion. Perhaps it is just shown...? Is the word LOVE necessary?

(Thought)

_____

_____

_____

_____

_____

_____

Thoughts and Quotes While Digging my Hands into the Earth
- Natural order of things are completely out of order once the unnatural order of things becomes accepted as natural.

- If wild is natural, then what is unnatural...?

(Thought)

_____

_____

_____

_____

_____

_____

—

Do you think you've fully bloomed?

All those who have testified or believe they have fully bloomed, may you'll rest in peace (R.I.P.)... I am damn sure nobody has ever fully bloomed and lived to talk about it; we just keep blooming until we fall...

(Thought)

_____

_____

_____

_____

_____

_____

Is time alive? Is it unfair? Is it a dictator? Is it an indicator of thing? Is it all things? Do it belong to anyone? Is it a gift? Who are we to label it or give it a name?

Is it free?

What is time?

(Thought)

_____

_____

_____

_____

_____

_____

Yesterday I had a day whereas peace was still and thoughts was fluid like water...but also chilly, as winter's rain...but much appreciated like the birth of my first born. Revelations.... in simplistic form...I saw myself last evening. Good morning!

Revelations that shows you yourself can be both chilling and warm....Share a chilling and warm moment or self-discovery... What was your thought?

(Thought)

_____

_____

_____

_____

_____

_____

There's a silent but organized loudness that whispers what time it is...it controls one's orientation & emotions...at some point in time folks must restructure their respective system... control emotions, understand orientations, and get tired of the silent but organized loudness telling them what time it is.

Do you agree or disagree? Explain.

(Thought)

_____

_____

_____

_____

_____

_____

A Muslim women asking Christian women back the same exact questions that Christian women asked of Muslim women...

Do you find it impossible to give up pork? Does it say not to eat pork in your holy book? Do you feel oppressed? Do you like wearing modest clothes? Do you feel like you want to drink alcoholic beverages? Do you have a college education? Do you know who Jesus is? Do you worship anyone or anything other than God or any of God's creations? Do you date? Do you get hot when you're overdressed? Does praying multiple times a day seem bothersome or extreme? Does your husband beat you? Do your religion obligate husbands to be responsible for maintaining food, clothing, and shelter? Have your husband ever loved other women? Do you hate covering your body? Do you believe in premarital sex? Are you Okay? Do you believe in all the tenants of your religion? Moreover, do you try and follow them?

(Answer / Thought)

_____

_____

_____

_____

_____

_____

I was here...

Ain't no buildings or highways being named after me...no street signs or flagpole lights with my name on it....but I was here. No the world didn't stop. No holidays or half days, banks stayed open, nothing on the news channel... but I was here.

Knia
Was
Here

A Birthday Haiku for Knia

Yellow in the sky.
Seventeen birthday balloons
for you, my sunshine.

Note Your Thoughts & Emotions

Note Your Thoughts & Emotions

Note Your Thoughts & Emotions

Note Your Thoughts & Emotions

Note Your Thoughts & Emotions

Note Your Thoughts & Emotions

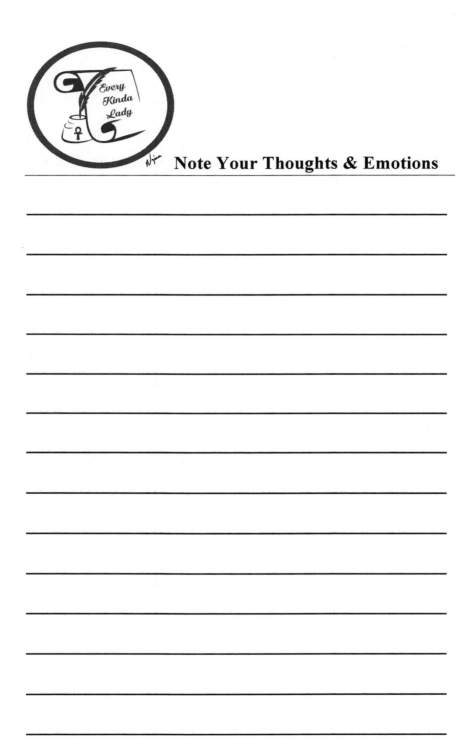

Note Your Thoughts & Emotions

Note Your Thoughts & Emotions

Note Your Thoughts & Emotions

Note Your Thoughts & Emotions

Note Your Thoughts & Emotions

Note Your Thoughts & Emotions

Note Your Thoughts & Emotions

Note Your Thoughts & Emotions

Note Your Thoughts & Emotions

Note Your Thoughts & Emotions

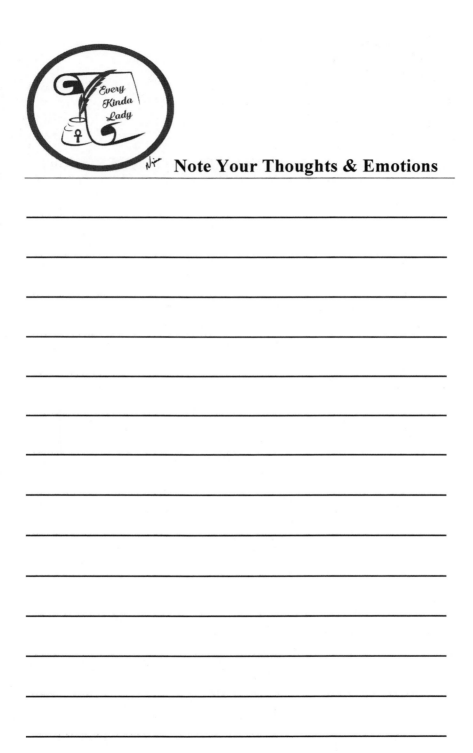

Note Your Thoughts & Emotions

Note Your Thoughts & Emotions

Note Your Thoughts & Emotions

Note Your Thoughts & Emotions

Note Your Thoughts & Emotions

Note Your Thoughts & Emotions

Note Your Thoughts & Emotions

Note Your Thoughts & Emotions

Note Your Thoughts & Emotions

Note Your Thoughts & Emotions

Note Your Thoughts & Emotions

Note Your Thoughts & Emotions

Note Your Thoughts & Emotions

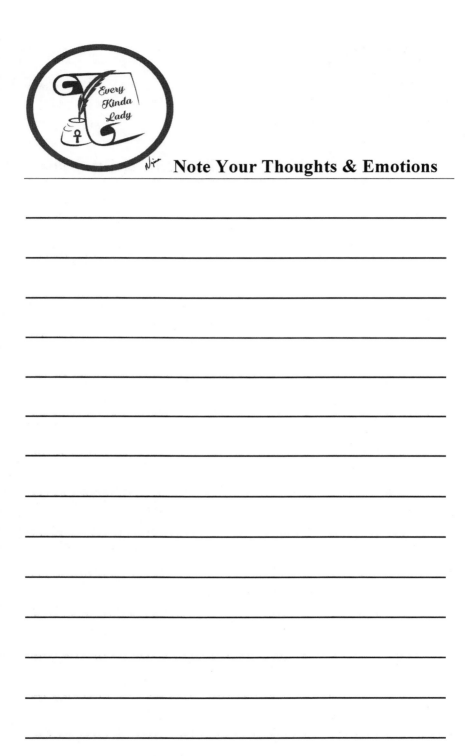

Note Your Thoughts & Emotions

Note Your Thoughts & Emotions

Note Your Thoughts & Emotions

Note Your Thoughts & Emotions

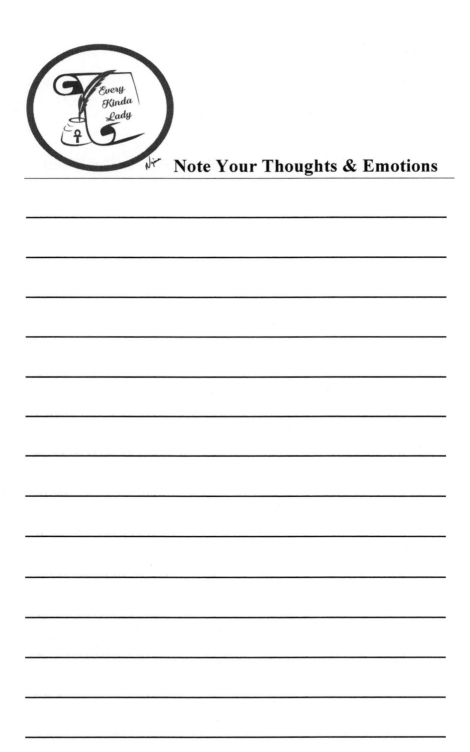

Note Your Thoughts & Emotions

Note Your Thoughts & Emotions

Note Your Thoughts & Emotions

Note Your Thoughts & Emotions

Note Your Thoughts & Emotions

Note Your Thoughts & Emotions

Note Your Thoughts & Emotions

Note Your Thoughts & Emotions

Note Your Thoughts & Emotions

Note Your Thoughts & Emotions

Note Your Thoughts & Emotions

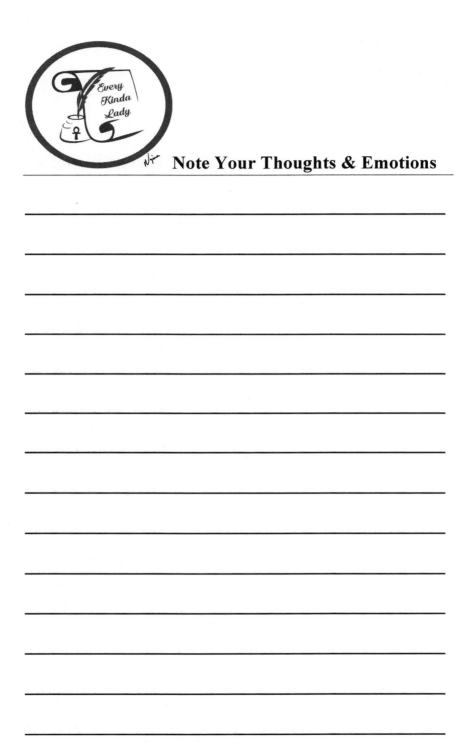

Note Your Thoughts & Emotions

Note Your Thoughts & Emotions

Note Your Thoughts & Emotions

Note Your Thoughts & Emotions

Note Your Thoughts & Emotions

Note Your Thoughts & Emotions

Note Your Thoughts & Emotions

Note Your Thoughts & Emotions

Note Your Thoughts & Emotions

Note Your Thoughts & Emotions

Note Your Thoughts & Emotions

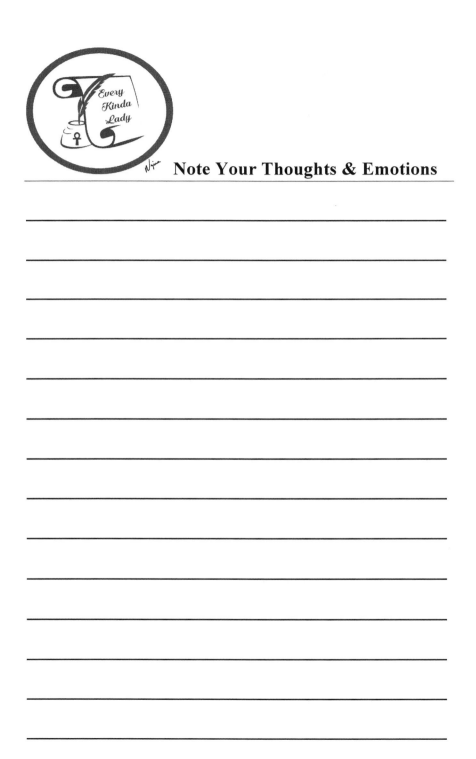

Note Your Thoughts & Emotions

Note Your Thoughts & Emotions

Note Your Thoughts & Emotions

Note Your Thoughts & Emotions

Note Your Thoughts & Emotions

Note Your Thoughts & Emotions

Note Your Thoughts & Emotions

Note Your Thoughts & Emotions

Note Your Thoughts & Emotions

Note Your Thoughts & Emotions

Note Your Thoughts & Emotions

Note Your Thoughts & Emotions

Note Your Thoughts & Emotions

Note Your Thoughts & Emotions

Note Your Thoughts & Emotions

A Special Thanks ...

A Moment of Silence (part 1)
I love you all and I am eternally grateful... Shakira G., Tanya F., Lolita G., Roni W., Tracy W., Cheresse H, Joy W., Yasmin A., Marisol R-C, Raschinna S., Linda G., Marguerite M., Demetria L.,Sherida S., Ashley H., Tatyana M., Teadra H., Manasia H., Josselyne H., Kimberly C., Chris H., Andre R., Sean H., Kejuan G., Chaz C., the Dumont family and the Kamara family...

A Moment of Silence (part 2)
*My angel princess looked lovely...*Shakira Greene & Tanya Fleeting, thank you for dressing my baby and fixing her hair and makeup, running town to town and doing everything I could never have done...and Nicole Roberson for picking out the style of her dress and headpiece...

"God Why my Flower Child" was first published in 2009 in *Freshwater Poetry Journal*, under my former name, Sherylle Roberson Hutchings

"Our Story" is revised. The original is published untitled in *Nota Bene* 2010 Phi Theta Kappa Honor Society Anthology, under my former government name, Sherylle Hutchings.

Special Acknowledgements and Gratitude

Dr. Mulazimuddin S. Rasool
As editor, contributor, & motivator…
I could not have done this book without you. Your patience and honesty is greatly appreciated.

Warm Appreciation & Love to my Family
To my immediate family who lives with me, thank you for being patient and supportive. To Na'Imah Muhammad, for being an amazing, giving and understanding Sister-friend.

Special Dedications

Stanley L. Shepard
My dad, for being my hero. Thank you for being an excellent father…

Knia K.Hutchings
To my Sunshine, my Flower Child, rest in peace. Thank you for giving life your best and for showing me what that truly mean. From Allah we come and to Allah we return…missing you.

All Praises be for
Allah

There's a difference between a women and a lady...

If you don't know the difference, I can't help you.

Made in the USA
Middletown, DE
28 July 2017